Python for Data Science

*The Ultimate Beginners' Guide to
Data Science, Predictive Analytics,
Statistics, and Machine Learning*

Zed Fast

Table of Contents

Introduction

Congratulations on purchasing *Python for Data Science,* and thank you for doing so.

The following chapters will discuss all of the information that we need to know in order to go through your own data science project. There are a lot of options that we are able to work with when it comes to data science, and almost all businesses are going to be able to handle this kind of process and see some of the benefits. If you have been wanting to know more about your customers and what they are looking for from you and your business, then the data science process is going to be the best option to help you out.

To start out this guidebook, we are going to take a look at what data science is all about, why it is important, and why we would want to work with this process in the first place as well. We will then take some time in order to learn the lifecycle of data science, and how we need to go through a series of steps like the finding the right data, preparing the data, coming up with the right model, and more. All of this and more will be discussed in this guidebook so that you can go from start to finish with your own data science project.

Then we are going to spend some time taking a look at the basics that come with the Python language, and how we are able to use this to help with our data science project. There are a lot of great coding languages out there that we are able to work with when it is time to handle data science, but many agree that the power, the libraries, and the ease to use and learn of Python make it one of the best choices to handle with this idea. We will also spend some time looking at a few of the libraries that are going to work with when it comes to Python, including NumPy and its arrays, Seaborn, and Matplotlib to get all of the work done in no time.

This is just the start of some of the amazing things that we are able to do when it is time to start on data science. We are able to spend our time looking at what machine learning is all about, the different types of machine learning, and how we are able to put it all together to makes sure that we can create the right algorithms and models when it is time to sort through our data and find the right patterns and insights in the process.

Then we can move on to the idea of predictive analysis. This is similar to what we see along with the data science process that we have talked about so far, but you will find that there are some key differences that show up as well. This method though is meant to take the data and use it specifically to ensure that we understand the results and that we can see the best predictions for what is going to happen if we take certain courses of action.

To finish off this guidebook, we are going to spend some time looking at some of the basics of data mining and how this fits into the whole process of data science that we are talking about here. And then, we will explore some of the different applications that we are going to work with when it is time to handle data and how companies all throughout the world, in a lot of different industries, are going to be able to handle data and use this whole process as well.

There are a lot of benefits that we are able to see when it comes to working on data science, and many companies in a lot of different industries are going to work with this in order to ensure that we will be able to handle how to work with their customers, how to beat out the competition, and so much more. When you are ready to work with the idea of data science, and you want to work with all of the different parts that are found with it, then make sure to check out this guidebook to help you get started.

There are plenty of books on this subject on the market, thanks again for choosing this one! Every effort was made to ensure it is full of as much useful information as possible; please enjoy it!

Chapter 1: What is Data Science?

Data science is likely a term that you have heard about at least a few times. If you are running a company, and you have ever taken a look at some of the steps that you are able to take in order to make yourself more efficient and to reduce the risks that you are experiencing when it is time to make some big and important decisions, then you have most likely heard about data science from others who are in the same boat as you. But this doesn't really explain that much about data science and what we are able to do with it. And that is where this guidebook is going to come into play.

As the world started to enter the era of big data, the need for the right storage to use with it was something else that seemed to grow like crazy as well too. This was actually one of the main challenges and concerns that happen with these industries, at least until a few years ago. The main focus because of this issue was that companies might be able to collect and use a lot of data for their needs, they didn't have a good place to store all of that data to work with later.

Now, thanks to some of the changes that are there in the technology that we have, this is no longer the big issue that it was in the past. And this means that we are able to make a few adjustments and work with more and more data in the process. And you will find that the secret sauce that is going to bring it all together and helps us to not only gather up the data that we need but will ensure that we are actually able to learn what is found in all of that data is going to be data science.

There are a lot of companies that are looking to get into the world of data science because they know all of the benefits that come with this as well. When we are ready to handle some of the data that is going on with all of this, we need to make sure that we are getting the right data, and that we actually understand all of the information that we are dealing with at the same time. But that is all going to be covered in the data analysis that we are doing along the way.

Why is Data Science So Important

The first thing that we need to take a look at when we are doing some of our work here is why data science is so important, and why a company may need to work with the process of data science along the way. The first issue is the way that this data has been structured in our modern world, especially when it is compared to how it was done in the past. Traditionally, the data that companies were able to get their hands on was going to be smaller in size, and it was pretty much structured the whole time. This allowed us to work with simple business intelligence tools in order to analyze what is going on.

However, this is not the case any longer. There are benefits and negatives that come with this, of course. It allows us the option to really know more about a situation because we are able to really gather up the data and understand more with more data. But often this data is going to be unstructured, and that makes it harder to sort through and understand as well.

Unlike some of the data that was found in those traditional systems, the ones that were structured and easier to work with, today, we will find that most of our data is unstructured or at least semi-structured. This is going to make it harder to work with and can take longer. But because we are able to find more information to help shape the decisions that we are making, this is not necessarily a bad thing all of the time.

This data is going to be generated from a lot of different sources, including things like instruments, sensors, multimedia forms, text files, and even some financial logs along the way. Because of all these sources that we are getting the data from, it is important to see that we are not able to work with some of the simple business intelligence tools because they are not going to be capable of handling all of this data and the variety of data as well. this is why it is important to work with data science in order to work with algorithms and analytical tools that are more advanced and complex as well. This ensures that we are able to really analyze and processes meaningful insights out of the data as well.

Of course, this is not going to be the only reason that data science is something that has become so popular. Let's dig deeper and see how data science is being used in a lot of different domains. For example, what if we are able to go through the data that we have, and we were then able to learn the precise requirements of the customers we have, using a lot of the data that we have on these existing customers. This could include things like their income, age, purchase history, and past browsing history, as well.

No doubt, you have been working with this kind of data already. But this doesn't mean that we had the right tools in order to handle some of this and get it all organized. With the work of data science, though, it is possible to train up the models in the most efficient manner and have some good precision when it is time to recommend products to your customers. And all of this can be done with data science when you get started.

Another situation where we are able to work with data science is how it is able to come into play with decision making. How about if you had a car that held onto the intelligence to make sure you can drive home. These cars are going to be useful because they will help us drive home or to any location where we would like with the help of sensors, radars, cameras, and lasers in order to create a map of what is around it.

Based on all of the data that the car is able to gather, it is going to be able to make decisions to help it drive, including when it should speed up or go slower when it should overtake another car, or even where to turn. With the help of data science and making use of advanced machine learning algorithms.

And we can even work with the idea of data science in order to help out with the predictive analytics. For example, we are able to work with something like weather forecasting. Data from things like satellites, radars, aircraft, ships, and more are able to be analyzed in order to help us build up some of the models that we have. These models are going to be useful when we are able to forecast the weather, while also being able to predict the occurrence of any natural calamities that we would like. It is also going to help us to take some of the right measures ahead of time when we see this, and can, in the process, help us save a lot of lives as well.

What is Data Science?

The next thing that we are able to look at is more about how data science is going to work. You will find that a lot of companies are going to use data science, and its use is going to become more common as time goes on. But what does this really mean in the long run? What are some of the skills that we will need to use in order to turn our careers into a data scientist? And what is the difference between the data science that we are talking about and business intelligence that was used in the past? And how are these predictions and decisions made in data science in the first place? All of these questions and more are going to be what we are able to explore when it comes to working with data science.

But before we go that far, we need to make sure that we learn more about data science. Data science is simply going to be a blend of a lot of algorithms, tools, and principles of machine learning. and the goal of using all of these is to discover some of the hidden patterns that are in the raw data.

You will find that there are also some differences that show up between a data scientist and a data analysis as well. The data analyst is going to spend time explaining what is going on with the data simply by taking the time to process the history of the data. Then there is the data scientist who is not going to just do an exploratory analysis in order to figure out what predictions and insights are found inside, but it is also going to work with a lot of algorithms of machine learning that are more advanced in order to help figure out how likely it is that an event is going to happen in the future.

During this process, there are a lot of different steps that the data scientist is going to need to do to see results.

For example, this individual is going to spend a lot of time looking at the data, and they will often do this from a lot of angles. The more angles that the data scientist is able to look at when it is time to handle this process, the more they are able to learn in the process.

So, you will find that data science is going to be used, for the most part, to help a company make important decisions, and even some predictions, with the help of a few different things, machine learning, prescriptive analytics, and even predictive causal analytics. Let's take a look at how each of these will work when they are combined with one another.

To start with, we are going to come with the idea of predictive causal analytics. If you would like to work with one of the models that are able to make some predictions and find out the possibility of whether an event is going to happen in the future or not, then the predictive causal analytics is going to be one of the options that you can choose. If you are a bank and you would like to provide someone with money on credit, then the probability of the customers making these payments in the future is going to be a big concern for what you are able to do in the process.

Of course, you will need to first create a model to help with this. This model, when it is time to work with it, will be able to perform some of the predictive analytics on the history of that customer's payments and then will help us predict whether or not this same customer will be able to make future payments on time or not.

Then we are able to move on to prescriptive analytics. If you would like to work with a model that has the intelligence to take its own decisions and the ability to go through and modify it with some parameters that are more dynamic, then this is the type of analytics for it. This is going to be a newer field of data science, and it is all about providing advice. Another way to look at this is that it is going to provide us with some advice and it is not only going to make predictions, but will suggest a range of actions that you should take, and the outcomes that are most likely to happen with this.

We can't have much of a discussion about data science and what comes with it without spending some time looking at machine learning and all of the parts that can come with this one as well. To start with, we are going to be able to use machine learning to make some good predictions. If you are working with some transactional data in the world of finances, and you would like to be able to take some of that information and build up a good model that will help us to determine where the trends will go in the future, then the algorithms of machine learning are going to be the best for you to use.

This is going to fall under the idea of supervised learning. The reason that it is known as supervised is that if you already have the data based on which you are able to train the machines, then you are supervising how it is going to work overall. For example, you may set up a model for fraud detection, and then you can train it with the use of a historical record of purchases that were fraudulent to start with.

And then there is a second way that we are able to work with machine learning when it comes to data science. And this is where we are going to use machine learning and some of the benefits that come with this in order to help out with pattern discovery. If you are set up to get going on this process, but you do not have the parameters to base your model on or which you can use to make the predictions, then it is time to find out the hidden patterns that are found within that option as well. This is nothing but the unsupervised learning of machine learning because you are not going to head into this process with any predefined labels that you would like to group along the way. The most common algorithm that you are able to work with on this one, though there are a lot of options available, will be clustering.

We can take a look at how we can make this work, for example, you may work for a telecommunications company, and it is your job to set up a new network in a region. You also have to figure out the best places to put up some towers in the region. You would want to gather up all of the information that you have at the time, and then use clustering in order to figure out the best places to put these towers so that they will serve the most people in the process.

There are a lot of benefits that come with working on a data science project for some of our own needs, and you will get the benefit of picking out from a lot of methods and techniques in order to see some of the results that you would like. When you handle some of the steps that we see above, you will find that this is going to be one of the best ways that we are able to take all of that data that we have been collecting for the long term, and then using it in a manner that really benefits our business as a whole.

This is definitely a process that anyone is able to work with, but it is not going to be quick or simple all of the time. We need to be able to learn how to make this work and some of the different steps that are necessary to see the right results. When you are ready to get started with the idea of data science and some of the steps that are necessary to make this happen, and then we can see just how this kind of process is going to benefit us the most.

Chapter 2: The Benefits of Python Data Science

There are a lot of great coding languages that you are able to spend your time working with. Each of then will be able to help us work with a different type of programming. Some work best with helping with gaming, and some work best with helping to work on websites and other things that need to be done online. But you will find that when you want a good language that is able to handle a lot of different options of coding and more, then you will find that Python is going to be one of the best options for you to choose.

There are a lot of benefits that are going to come with working on Python, especially when it is time to work with some of the things that you need in data science. We are going to spend some time here looking at some of the benefits of data science and how we are able to work with this language to get to our goals here.

The first benefit that is done when it comes to working with the Python language is that it is easy to learn how to work with. There are a lot of beginners who have never been able to do anything in coding in the past, and they worry that it is going to be too hard to work with. They decide to put it off, and then they end up not working with some of the things they want with data science and more because of that.

This is no longer an issue when you are working with the Python language. You will find that this language was designed in order to handle some of the codings that you would like. It is designed as a language that is able to handle the beginner, it is written out in English, and just by taking a look at a few of the codes that are in Python, before you even learn how to use it.

The good news here, though, is that even though this is an easier language to learn compared to some of the other options, it is going to come with all of the power that you are looking for along the way as well. Many people worry that because this is supposed to be a language for beginners, it is going to be too simple to handle some of the more complicated things that we are working within coding. But this is not something that we need to work with at all when it comes to the Python language.

In fact, Python has the strength to handle a lot of the different things that you would like to get done, no matter what kind of coding you would like to do. With the help of a few libraries and extensions that are able to be added to the Python language, you will find that this is going to be able to handle things like machine learning, data science, and so much more. All of the power that we need is going to be found when it is time to work with this language.

Another benefit of working with this language is that it is considered an OOP language. These OOP languages are based on classes and objects, which is going to help us to really keep things organized in the manner that we would like, and will ensure that we are going to be able to put it all together and find what we would like. This is a feature of some of the newer languages that are out there, and it really makes learning and using the codes that we would like so much easier.

Python also has a lot of different libraries that you are able to work with, from the basic standard library that is great for helping you learn how to code all the way to the more complicated libraries that are going to ensure you can get your tasks done. There are a lot of extensions out there that we are able to handle, and you are able to add on any of the libraries that are needed to get the work done in no time.

There is also the benefit of being able to utilize the large community that comes with Python when things get tough or when you get stuck and can't make something work the way that we would like. Because this is such a great language to work with, and it is going to help us out with so many of the options that we are able to handle when it is time to start coding, there is a large community out there that we are able to handle all of the things that you would like to do. You will be able to find a large number of programmers from professionals and more, in order to make sure that we get the best results overall.

As a beginner, you are going to find that this community is a great option for us to work with. You will find that this community will be able to teach you some new things in order to get started, can answer some of the questions that you are working with, and even help you when some of the codings get tough and you are not certain how to make it all work overall.

And finally, we are going to find that the Python language is compatible with other languages. For the most part, you will be able to work with just the Python language, and it will be able to handle all of the work that you need along the way. But there are some cases, especially when it comes to working with data science and more, that you will need to combine together a few of the other languages that are out there with the Python language.

This is something that is really easy to do, and some of the libraries that you will use with data science will allow you to do this. They can make it easy to type in your code in Python, and then the library will take that and execute it in another language if you would like. Python is really versatile, and you will find that it will help us to work with other languages as we would need.

As we can see, there are a lot of benefits that we are able to work with when it is time to use the Python language in order to see some of the great results that are needed along the way. When you decide to work with the Python language, you will find that it is going to be able to work well with handling all of the algorithms and models that we want to handle throughout this process, and it can even be a good option when you need to find and organize the data that we are working with as well. When you are ready to get through and work on the data science process, then you will be able to work with the Python language as well.

Chapter 3: The Lifecycle of Data Science

The next thing that we need to take a look at here is the lifecycle of data science. There are actually quite a few steps that we need to focus on here in order to make sure that we are going to get the most out of any data science project that we are trying to work with along the way. It would be nice if it were a process that just took a few minutes, and then we were set, but this is just not how things are meant to go.

There are a lot of steps that have to all come together and work well together to ensure that this is going to work in the manner that we would like. You have to make sure that you have the right data, for example, you have to make sure that you clean out the data and get it organization, and you need to run it through the algorithms and other models that you would like, just to learn what information and insights are found in all of that data.

This is a complex process that is going to take some time to accomplish, and often those who are just getting started with this process are going to be amazed at the amount of work that they have to use in order to make this happen for their needs. Knowing the steps ahead of time will ensure that you are able to really get the most out of this process, that you will start out and end up in the right spot, and so much more. With that in mind, some of the steps that we need to use in order to get started with doing our own process of data science will include:

The Discovery Phase

The first phase of this that we need to take a look at is going to be the discovery phase. This is going to include a lot of questions, a lot of research, and a good understanding of what your business is hoping to get out of this whole process before we even get started. Before you even think about starting out on this project, it is important to go through and understand some of the different specifications, the requirements, and then the priorities and required the budget to make this all work.

Going in without all of this in place is just going to lead to a mess. If you do not have an idea of what the specifications and priorities are supposed to be in this process, then you are just going to grab any random data that you can find, and that is easy to gather up, and then call it good. This will definitely not be a good thing for what you are trying to do. If you do not go into this knowing the budget, the money will run out way before you are able to figure out how this process even works.

You need to make sure in this stage that you have the right ability in order to ask the right questions all of the time. Here, you will assess if you have the right resources at hand, as well. This means that you need to know whether you have the right amount of data, time, technology, and people in order to fully support the project that you are working with. And finally, we have to be able to frame our main business problem (or at least the one that we want to work with right now) and formulate an initial hypothesis to test it all out.

The Data Preparation Phase

The next thing that we need to take a look at is the data preparation phase. This is going to be the phase where you will spend most of your time in because we have to make sure that we are not just gathering up the right information as we go along. We want to make sure that we are organizing the data, dealing with the outliers that are there, filling in the missing values, and being careful about the duplicates that are going to show up in this process as well. It is a difficult task to work with, but it is necessary if we would like to make sure that our predictions are going to be as accurate as possible.

This is not the most glamorous out of the work that you are doing, but it is very important. In this phase, it is often necessary that we have an analytical sandbox in which we are able to perform some of the analytics for the entire time that we work on the project at hand. We need to spend some time in this stage looking at exploring the data, preprocessing it, and conditioning the data before we do the modeling.

This all takes time, and it may not be fun, but it is something that is necessary when it comes to the success of your project. In addition, during this phase, we are going to work with the process known as ETLT, or extract, transform, load, and transform in order to make sure that the data is organized and ready to go in the manner that we would like, and to make sure that we are able to get the data into the sandbox that we would like.

There are going to be a few different options that we are able to work in order to handle the data preparation phase that we are on right now. The two most popular options and the ones that will ensure that we are able to get the most out of the process will be the R and the Python coding language. For the most part, data scientists are going to use Python in order to get the most out of their training process.

For all of the reasons that we talked about in the previous chapter, working with Python is the best choice. It is simple enough to learn how to use, even for someone who is more of a beginner in all of this, and it will ensure that you have all of the power and all of the libraries that are needed in order to handle this phase as well.

There are a lot of different parts that we are going to focus on when it is time to handle the data preparation phase of the whole process. And often, it is a phase that we are not going to spend enough time on. But in reality, if the data that you have is not organized and ready to go in the manner that you would like, then it is going to cause a lot of problems along the way.

The cleaner that you are able to make that data, the better. When the data is higher in quality, and when things like the outliers, duplicates, and missing values are gone, it is so much easier to work with all of this. The algorithm will be able to go through the data more efficiently than before, and you will predictions and insights that you are actually able to handle and trust along the way as well.

The Model Planning Phase

The third step that we are going to be able to work with is known as the model planning phase. In this one, we are going to spend some time determining the techniques and methods that are available in order to draw up the relationships between the variables that we have. These relationships are important because they are basically going to help us set the foundation for the algorithms that we want to implement. Without these algorithms, your coding is not going to work, and you will never learn what is inside of that data you are dealing with. And we will learn how to implement some of these algorithms in the next phase.

There are a number of planning tools that are available for us to work with on this one. Most programmers are going to focus on the Python language and all of the benefits that it is able to provide. There are a few others that we are able to spend our time and attention on, and these will include:

1. R: This one is sometimes seen as the best option to work with when it comes to completing a data analysis because it allows us to have the capabilities of modeling and will provide us with a really good environment when it is time to build up the interpretive models that we want.

2. SQL Analysis services: These are going to be the ones that are able to perform some of the analytics that needs to happen in the database. These are going to be done thanks to some of the more common functions of data mining, as long as they are used with some of the basic predictive models that you need as well.

3. SAS/ACCESS: This one is going to be helpful because we are able to use it to access all of the data that we need from the Hadoop system when we need it the most. And it is often going to be used when we would like to create model flow diagrams that we can repeat, and that we are able to reuse in the process as well.

At this point, we should have a really good idea about some of the nature of our data, and we should know whether it is to the quality standards that we are looking for or not. And because of this, it is time to move on to the next step and ensure that we are ready to handle some of the data by putting it through the algorithms that we pick in the next step.

This is where we are heading in the next step as well. it will be time to add in a bit of machine learning (which we are going to be able to use in more depth later on when we discuss it), in order to find a good algorithm that will go through the data that we have, and will provide us with the insights and predictions that we need. But this is only going to happen when we are able to go through and do some of the steps that were listed out before.

The Model Building Phase

The fourth step that we need to take some time on here is going to be the model-building phase. When we are here, we will need to actually go through and use the machine learning and some of the algorithms that are necessary with it and put it to good use. This is also the phase where we are going to find all of the data sets and more that we need to handle the training and the testing.

One thing that a lot of people are not aware of when they first get started with all of this is that they actually need to go through and train and then test the algorithm. They assume that they are able to just write out the algorithm in the manner that they would like, and then put through the data that they want. They then assume that the data that comes out of these untrained and untested algorithms are going to be accurate and will actually help them out with the work that they want to do.

But these algorithms have to be trained in some manner, and if you do not take the time to do this training ahead of time, or you don't take the time to test them out either, then you are going to end up with some trouble. The algorithm is not going to be as accurate as we would like, and we will end up with a lot of predictions and insights that we are not able to trust at all.

During this phase, we will also need to take some time to discover or consider whether the tools that we already have in our possession are going to be enough to help run some of those models, or if we are going to need to make sure that the environment that we are working with will be more robust. Usually, when we take a look at this, we are interested in finding out whether the processing power that we have is strong enough to handle the work or if we need to change it up.

The good news here is that there are a lot of great algorithms that we are able to use to make this one work, and when we are able to put them all together and use all of the tools that are out there, you will be able to create some really good information that will push you forward. But you have to take the time to really optimize the algorithm that you want to work with and to ensure that it is going to be able to handle some of the predictions and insights that we need to make all of this work for our needs.

The Operationalize Phase

When we are working with this phase, it is time to deliver some of the final reports and briefings, as well as some of the codes and technical documents that are needed to go along with this one. Usually, the data scientist will need to spend their time showing the right people in the business how to work on the information and make it work for their needs as well. And since a lot of these key decision-makers are often not going to have technical backgrounds so understanding the information is going to be tough.

This is why the data scientist will need to spend some time going through the information and getting it set up in a manner that will make it easier overall. When the data is turned into a format that we are able to understand, and will ensure that those who are using the information for making decisions, then it is going to help them out quite a bit.

In addition, sometimes we are going to take some time to work on a pilot project. This can be implemented in real-time in the production environment as well. This allows us to take some time to try out some of the insights that we have found, without having to implement it throughout the whole company. This gives us a better idea of what is going on with some of the work that we are doing, and to see whether the process we want to use is going to actually work before we waste time and money on doing it throughout the company. This is one of the best ways for us to go through and see a clear picture of the performance and other related constraints on a smaller scale before you deploy it completely.

The Communicate Results Phase

At this point, it is important for us to go through and evaluate whether or not we have been able to achieve some of our goals. This is talking about some of the goals that we were able to go through in the first phase of this process. If we have not been able to gather up and work with the goals along the way, then we will be able to work with making some of the necessary changes that will help us to meet our goals.

So, when we are in this last phase, we are going to spend some time identifying all of the key findings that are going to show up along the way. And when we have been able to identify some of these key findings, we can then communicate that information between the stakeholders, and then determine whether or not the results of this project are going to be a failure, or if we were successful. But we have to base all of this off the criteria that we took the time to develop and look at in the first phase.

As we can see, there is quite a bit that is going to show up when it is time to handle some of the work that we need with a data science project. We have to go through all of these phases to ensure that we are going to see some of the best results along the way. And when it all comes together, we will be able to have the right data, that we are cleaning it off, and that we are picking out the right algorithms to ensure that this is going to work the way that we would like.

Chapter 4: Manipulating Our Arrays

Now it is time for us to take a look at how we are able to work with some of the arrays that are in our midst and how these are going to be important to unlocking some of the power that we are going to be able to work with when it comes to the arrays and the NumPy library.

Like many of the other data science libraries that are out there and will work with Python as well, NumPy is going to be one of the packages that we just can't miss out on when it is time to learn more about data science along the way. This is because NumPy is going to be able to provide us with some of the data structure that we need with arrays that will hold a few benefits over the list with Python. For example, the arrays are going to be more compact, they can access faster when it is time to read and write the items, and they are more efficient and convenient to work with overall.

With this in mind, we are going to spend some time looking at how to work with the NumPy arrays. We are going to look at how to work with these, how they can be installed, and even how to make some of the arrays that we would like to work with, even when you need to work with the data when it is on the files.

The NumPy Array

The first thing that we are going to take a look at here is the NumPy array. The arrays that come from this library are going to be similar to the lists that we are going to find in Python, but there are some differences that are going to show up. The array is going to be one of the central structures of data that are found in the NumPy library. In other words, the NumPy library is going to be one of the core libraries that we need to work with when it is time to do some scientific computing, and the arrays are going to be central to getting things done in this library as well.

When we take a look at the print of a few arrays, you are going to see that it is more of a grid that will hold onto values that are the same type. You will then see that the data is often going to be in integers. The array is going to help us out by holding and representing any regular data that has been structured in this manner.

However, we are going to be aware that, on a structural level, an array is basically going to be nothing but pointers. It is going to be a combination of the memory address, shapes, strides, and a data type. Some of the things that we need to know when we go through this process include:

1. The data pointer is going to be important in order to indicate the memory address that we are going to find with the first byte of this particular array.
2. Then we are able to work with the dtype, or the data type. This pointer is going to describe the kind of elements that we are able to find inside of the array that we are working with.
3. Then we move on to the shape. This is going to give us a better idea of the shape that our array is going to take.
4. And finally, we are on the strides. These will basically be the number of bytes that we are able to skip in the memory so that we can then go on to the next elements. So, if you end up with strides of (10, 1), you will need to proceed one byte in order to get to the next column, and 10 bytes so that they are in the next row.

To put this in other words, an array is going to be able to contain a lot of information about the data that is raw, how to find the element that we are able to work with, and how we are able to interpret the specific element that we would like to work with.

Now we are able to take this a bit further to see how it is going to work for some of our needs. We are able to easily test out this process by exploring some of the attributes that come with the NumPy array, and this can be done with some of the information below:

yJsYW5ndWFnZSI6InB5dGhvbiIsInByZV9leGVyY2lzZV

You can see with this one that there is going to be a lot more information that is going to show up when you click on this one. For example, the type of data that we are working with is going to be printed out and will be "int64" or signed 32-bit integer type. This is going to be much more detailed than we find before. This also means that we are going to store the array in memory as 64 bytes. This is because each integer is going to take up to 8 bytes, and you are going to work here with an array that has 8 integers.

The strides that we are going to see with the array are able to tell us that it is important for us to skip 8 bytes, which is one value here, to move to the next column when it is needed. But if we are working with the 32 bytes, which would be four values, to get to the same position in the next row. The strides that we would see with this kind of array is going to be (32, 4).

Note that if we set up the type of data on this one to be int32, then the strides tuple that you are able to get back is going to be (16, 4), as you will still just need to move one value to the next column and 4 values to get to the same potion. The only thing that we will need to change up here is the fact that all of the integers will take up 4 bytes rather than the 8 that you are expecting at this time.

As we can see, working with the arrays is pretty simple, but it is going to be important when it is time to handle some o the work that we are trying to do with our Python and with data science in the same process. When we are able to handle all of this at the same time and put it together, you will find that it works with a lot of options with the other data science libraries that we would like to work with as well.

Chapter 5: How Machine Learning Works for Data Science

The next topic that we need to spend some time on here is known as machine learning. Machine learning is an interesting option that is going to be able to work with data science to give us some of the information that we need. This option is going to have a network or system work based on experiences and examples, and that it is able to do all of this without being programmed on how to behave in every situation.

What this means is that instead of the programmer spending time writing out the codes they want, we will spend time feeding data into a generic algorithm. From there, the algorithm machine is going to be able to build up the logic based on the data that is given. There are a lot of parts that come with machine learning, and figuring out how we are able to work with this and more can really ensure that we get the most out of this along the way as well.

There are already a lot of applications where we are seeing machine learning growing so much. If you have ever worked with a search engine to find something online, then we are familiar with some of the work that we are able to do with machine learning. If you have worked with some kind of voice-activated device, whether it is on your phone or on one of those personal assistant devices, then you will find that you have worked with machine learning as well. And these are just the start of what we are able to do with machine learning as well.

In the future, it is likely that this technology is going to go into new industries and provide us with new products and technology that we can't imagine today. It is already able to do so many things for us, and when we think about the future of this technology, as more and more people jump on it and learn how to use it, we are sure to see some amazing things. With this in mind, let's take some time to learn a bit more about machine learning and how we are able to use this for our needs as well.

What is Machine Learning

Now it is time for us to take a look at some of the basics that are going to come with machine learning and how we are able to use this for our needs. Think about a few of the situations that you have done in the past. For example, have you ever spent time shopping online? While you were checking for some of the products that you want to purchase, did you ever notice when it would make recommendations for you, based on the product that you are looking at, or base don some of the purchases that you made in the past? If you have seen something similar to this on a website that you are shopping on, then you have been exposed to machine learning.

Another example is when you get a call from a bank or another financial company which will ask you to take out a new insurance policy or a loan. It is unlikely that this financial institution is going to waste their time calling everyone. This would take too long and would be a waste. Instead, they are going to use machine learning in order to help them figure out the best customers, the ones who are most likely to purchase their products before starting.

So, let's take a closer look at what machine learning is all about. Machine learning is basically going to be one of the parts of artificial intelligence that are going to focus mainly on machine learning from their experience.

Then the machine is able to make some predictions based on the experience that has happened in the past.

What does machine learning do? It is going to enable the system, machines, computers, and more to make decisions, decisions that are based on data, rather than having the programmer do all of the codings to get this done. These programs or algorithms are going to be designed in a different manner than what we find in the past because they are able to learn and improve over time when we have been able to expose them to some new data. This is what is going to make them so strong and good at analyzing the data that you are working with along the way.

As most of us know today, we are really in a world that involves both machines and humans at the same time. Humans, which are us, have been evolving and learning from our past experiences for millions of years since we came about. But we will find, on the other hand, that the era of robots and machines is one that is just beginning. You can consider it in a manner that we are living in the primitive age of machines, while the future of what these machines will be able to do is enormous and we are not able to imagine it at this point.

In the world that we work in today, these machines, or the robots, have to still be programmed before they are able to really start following any of the instructions that you would like. But what if, in the future, the machine is able to start learning on their own from work and experience as we do. This is not something that we are able to use right now, but it is an interesting part that we can consider to help us reach some of our goals with machine learning later on.

What Does Machine Learning Do?

The algorithms that we are able to use with machine learning will be trained, with the help of the data we set aside for training, in order to create the model that we would like. When we put in some new input data to this algorithm, it is going to use some of the models as its basis for providing us with some of the predictions that we need along the way.

The prediction that the algorithm is able to give for us is going to be evaluated for accuracy, and if we find that the accuracy is acceptable, then this algorithm with machine learning is going to be deployed. If we decide that the accuracy level is not good, then this algorithm will go through again and be trained until it reaches the accuracy that we would like.

There are a lot of ways that machine learning is going to be able to help us out. Many times the analysis part of our data science project is going to happen with machine learning, and that can really make a difference in the insights that we are going to find along the way as well. And with all of the great techniques and methods that we are able to use here as well will ensure that we are going to get the results that we need.

The Different Types of Machine Learning

The next thing that we need to spend some time on is the different types of machine learning that we are able to work with. There are three main types of machine learning that we are able to work with. These are going to include supervised learning, unsupervised learning, and reinforcement learning. We are going to take some time to look at each of these and see what we are able to do with each of them to help us reach our goals.

First, we need to take a look at what supervised learning is all about. When we are talking about supervised learning, we are talking about the one where we are able to use labeled data and examples in order to help the algorithm work. We can view this one like the algorithm being guided by a teacher. We are going to have a set of data that is going to act as the teacher, and the role of this teacher, or data set, is going to be the train the model or the machine that we are working with. Once we have been able to go through and train the model, we are able to use it to start making some predictions or decisions when the new data is provided to it later on.

Then we are able to work with the idea of unsupervised learning as well. This one is going to be a bit different than what we are used to with supervised learning, but it is going to add in some of the functionality that we are looking for when it is time to handle our work with machine learning. The models of unsupervised learning are going to learn through a lot of observations, and then, with the help of these observations, it is able to find some of the structures that we need in the data.

Once the model is given the set of data that we want to work with, it is automatically able to find some of the relationships and patterns that are in the set of data, usually through the process of creating clusters in it. What it is not able to do here is add in labels to the clusters at all. This means that it is not able to tell us that one group is apples and another is mangoes, but it is able to separate them out because they are quite a bit different.

Let's say that we had a bunch of images that we wanted to use mangoes, bananas, and apples. With the use of unsupervised learning, this is going to take a look at the relationships and patterns that are found in those images and will create some clusters while dividing up the set of data into those various clusters. If you find that the new data is fed into the model after it is all done, then it is going to take that new data and add it into one of the created clusters that you have.

And finally, we are able to work with the idea of reinforcement learning. On the outside of this, before we dive into it too much, we are going to find that reinforcement learning looks a lot like what we are going to see with the unsupervised learning that we talked about above. But the main difference is that reinforcement learning is going to rely more on the idea of trial and error to help the algorithm to learn.

Reinforcement learning is going to be the ability of the agent in order to interact with the environment in the hopes of figuring out what outcome is going to be the best. And, as we mentioned before, it is going to follow the idea of working with a trial and error method. The agent is going to be rewarded and sometimes penalized, with a point for a correct or a wrong answer. And on the basis of the positive reward points that are gained here, it is able to learn more than ever before. And again, once it is trained, it is going to get ready to predict some of the new data that is presented to it later on.

As we can see, there are a lot of parts that are going to come with the machine learning that we are able to work with. And this is going to be a really important option that we are able to focus on when it comes to data science. If you are looking to work on a data science project of any kind, and you need some models or algorithms that are going to help us to sort through the data and give us the insights and patterns that we need, then you have to spend some time working with the machine learning that we did before.

Chapter 6: What is Predictive Analysis?

Another thing that we need to spend some time on in this guidebook is the idea of predictive analysis. This is a great option to work with because it takes all of that data that we have been working with so far, and we use it to make some predictions on what we should do later on and what is the most likely outcome that will happen based on the other decisions that we have along the way.

To start with, predictive analysis is going to be when we are able to work with data, techniques of machine learning, and lots of statistical algorithms in order to figure out how likely it is that future outcomes are going to happen, based on some of the historical data that we can find. The goal that we are going to see with this one is to go beyond knowing what has happened in the past in order to figure out what is likely to happen in the future.

Why Is This Analysis Important?

We also need to take some time to look closely at why this kind of analysis is going to be so important. Many companies are already turning to this kind of analytics in order to help them solve some of the more difficult problems that they are facing and to ensure that they are able to uncover some of the new opportunities that will help them to get ahead.

For example, companies like to work with this kind of analysis in order to help them detect whether fraud is going on or not. When they are able to combine together multiple analytics methods, they are able to go through and improve pattern detection and even prevent some of this criminal behavior. For many companies, working with the prevention of fraud is going to save them a lot of money, and can ensure that their customers feel like they are safe using this company.

Another benefit that we are able to see when it comes to a predictive analysis is that it is able to optimize some of the marketing campaigns that they are using. Predictive analytics, like what we are talking about here, is going to be used in order to determine some of the customer responses or purchases, and it shows us a lot of the best cross-selling opportunities that are out there. Some of the predictive models that are available can help a business to attract, retain, and even grow some of their most profitable customers along the way, as well.

We will also see that this kind of analysis is going to work to improve the operations of many businesses as well. There are a lot of companies that are going to use these models in order to forecast inventory and help to manage their resources.

Airlines are able to work with these predictive analytics on a regular basis in order to set some of the ticket prices for the customers. And hotels are going to use it in order to figure out how many guests for a given night are actually going to show up in order to increase their revenues and maximize the occupancy rate that is there. When these industries work with things like predictive analytics, it is going to help them to function in a more efficient manner overall

And finally, we will see that this predictive analytics is going to be great when it comes to reducing the amount of risk that the company is going to take on. For example, things like credit scores are going to be used in order to figure out the likelihood of a particular customer defaulting on some of their purchases, and they are also a good example of this predictive analytics. A credit score may seem kind of arbitrary in many cases, but it is going to be one of the predictive models that we are able to use that helps to incorporate all of the relevant data that is needed on the creditworthiness of the customer.

How This Works

The next thing that we are able to take a look at is how these predictive analysis is going to work. The models here are going to use known results in order to train or develop the model that we want, one that is able to be used to predict values for new or different data. This modeling is going to provide us results in the form of predictions that are going to represent the probability of the target variable, which can be revenue in some cases. This is going to be done based on the estimated significance from a set of input variables.

This is going to be a bit different than some of the descriptive models that are going to help us to understand what has happened, or some of the diagnostic models that will help us to understand why something happens or help to us to understand some of the key relationships that are showing up in our data as well. there are a lot of books and courses out there in order to help out with some of these analytical methods and techniques.

There are two options that we are able to work with when it comes to some of the predictive models that we are able to handle. These are going to include the classification models and the regression models. First, we are going to take a look at these classification models. These are going to be the ones that will help us to figure out, or make predictions about the membership of a class.

For example, you may try to use this in order to classify whether or not someone is likely to leave your company and not make purchases any longer, whether they are likely to respond to some of the marketing that you send to them, whether the customer is going to be seen as a good or bad credit risk and more. Usually, the model results are going to show up in the form of 0 and 1. 1 is going to be that the event is likely to happen, and 0 means that the situation is not likely to happen.

Then there are going to be the options that fit into the regression model. This is going to be the model that we are able to use in order to predict a number. For example, we could work with the regression models in order to see how much revenue a customer is going to generate over the next year, or how many months we will have before a component on a machine ends up failing.

The Steps of Predictive Analysis

Before we end with this chapter, we need to take a quick look at the steps that are going to come with doing predictive analysis. First, we want to figure out what problem we would like to solve. Think about what we would like to learn about and predict in the future based on information that we have in the past? You will also need to consider what you would like to do with some of these predictions when they are done. And what decisions you plan to make based on those insights as well.

Then we need to get the data that is necessary. In the world we are in today, this means that we need to go do some research in order to find the data from a lot of different sources transactional systems, sensors, information from other parties, notes on the call center, weblogs, web sites, and more are all places where you will need to collect data from in order to learn more about your customers and how you are able to find out more about how to serve them and provide them with a better customer experience.

You should consider having a good data wrangler here to get the work done. This will be useful to make sure that you are able to clean and prepare the data so that it is ready for the analysis that you would like to get done. And to make sure that the data is ready for the exercises for predictive modeling, you will need to work with someone who will understand the data and the business problem. How you are able to define your target is going to be so important when it is time to interpret the outcome that you will have.

The third step that we are going to be taking a look at is how to build up the predictive model as well. software that is getting easier to use all of the time is going to help us to build up some of the analytical models that we need. But you will still need to work with a professional in these data analysis in order to help refine the models and come up with the performer who is the best at this time.

And then, we may need to take this a bit further in order to make sure that this is going to work the best way that it can. For example, you may need to work with someone in your IT department in order to take the models that you were able to create and then deploy them and get them to work. That means that putting the models t work on some of the data that we have chosen, and that is where we are able to get the results that we want.

And finally, we are going to work with what is known as predictive modeling. This is going to be something that will require more of a team approach than other options. You need to work with people who are able to understand fully the business problem that you would like to solve. Someone who really knows how we are supposed to prepare the data to get through the analysis. And even someone who is able to build up and then refine some of the models that we are going to see. Adding in someone like an IT professional to ensure that you have the right analytics infrastructure for model building and even deployment. This will help us to get through the process as well and gives us some of the predictions that we are able to work with.

Chapter 7: The Importance of Visuals with Data Science

Another important part that we need to take a look at when it is time to handle some of our work with data science is the idea of the visuals. Let's say that we have been able to go through some of the steps that we listed out earlier. We picked out the data that we want to work with, and we know that it is going to be specific to some of the business problems that we would like to handle and take care of as well.

We have taken the time to clean and organize the data so that it is high-quality and ready to go. And we have worked with the Python language and machine learning in order to make some of the great algorithms that we need. And we have gone through and trained these algorithms and tested them, in order to make sure that we are able to rely on the information that we were able to get out of this process. And we even took the time in order to learn a bit more about the data, run it through our prepared algorithms, and even ensured that we could see what insights and predictions are going to come from all of this.

So, what is going to be the next step? We have gone through already, and we have figured out some of the insights that are there inside of all that data. But at this point, we are just looking at a bunch of facts and figures, and there isn't much else that is going to be found with it. These can be placed into reports and more. But you will find that this is going to be more difficult to work with overall, and sometimes reading that information and understanding what it says is going to be a bit more difficult to work with.

Of course, we could read through these spreadsheets and these reports and find out what information is inside of them. But this takes a lot of time and can be kind of tedious. And since many of the people who will actually work with this data and make decisions off this data, will not have a technical background for data science, it is going to be hard to understand.

This doesn't mean that all hopes are lost in the process. It just means that we need to take a different approach. And in many situations, we will find that working with visuals, charts, and graphs that are able to represent the data, can help us to see some of the more complicated relationships that are found in the data, whether we have that technical background or not.

This is going to really help us to get some of the best results when we are focusing on some of our work with data science. Since the human mind is going to be able to help us out more when we are looking at our data in the forms of a visual, rather than looking at it in lots of words and reports. We are able to glance down at the data and see it in a graph, helping us to understand what is there much faster, and more efficiently as well.

This is why we will spend some tie working with visuals when it is time to work with data science overall. Remember that we collected a ton of data in some of our first steps. This is going to be necessary so that we have enough information in order to handle the training, the testing, and then the actual use of the algorithms to provide you with the right predictions and insights overall. But you will find that all of this data is going to be complex.

Trying to read through the information is going to be important overall, but you will find that trying to get through the complex relationships when you have all of that data is going to be hard. And this is where the data visuals are going to be important as well. they can take all of that data, look through it, and put it into some kind of visual, usually something like a graph or chart that is easier to handle overall.

You have to be careful about the kind of visual that you are going to work with overall. There are a lot of choices that you are able to make here, but if you are not careful about this, you will pick the wrong visual, and you will not be able to go through and understand how the data works, or what it is trying to say to you. The right kind of visual is going to be important when it comes to handling your data, and taking the time to learn about the different types, and knowing a bit about your data in the first place, will ensure that you are able to really take a look at it and get the results that you want in no time as well.

There are a lot of options when it is time to pick out the visual that you would like to work with. We can work with things like pie charts, bar graphs, line graphs, histograms, and more. Each of these will be able to go through in order to show off the data that we are working with, but knowing more about the data is going to ensure that we pick one, and that those who need to make the most important decisions for their business based on that data will be able to understand it so much better.

Keep in mind with this one that we need to focus on the visuals and how they are able to make our life a little bit easier when we are doing this process; they are not always going to be able to handle everything. And this doesn't mean that we should ignore the reports and spreadsheets as well. these need to be there along with the visuals. This ensures that the people who are taking a look at the data are going to have the benefit of seeing what these are all about, and where you get your research from, and then you can move on from there as well. Having the reports and research together with one another, and the visuals as well in the mix, will ensure that we are going to really see the relationships in the data, and so much more.

There are a lot of benefits that we are able to see when it comes to working with data visuals, and you will find that working with one of these is going to be so important when it is time to finishing up the process of data science that we are focusing on here. There are a lot of parts that will come with the data science project, and adding in the visuals will be the part that we need to focus on in the end to ensure that we are not wasting time and that we are really able to work with the predictions that we need to see some of the best results along the way.

Chapter 8: How to Work with Matplotlib to Create Great Visuals

Another great library that we are able to work with, especially when we are spending some time working on our own visuals as we talked about before, is the matplotlib library. This is going to be a great option to work with when we handle some of the work that we want to do with a data science project, and will ensure that we are able to take all of the data points, and all of the different predictions that we were able to get with our algorithms and some of the machine learning hat we have from earlier, in order to help us with visuals so that we understand the data a little bit easier.

To start with, the Matplotlib is going to be one of the plotting libraries that is available to work along with the Python programming language. It is also going to be one of the components that come with the NumPy library that we talked about before, big data, and some of the numerical handling resources. Matplotlib uses an API that is more object-oriented in order to help embed plots in applications of Python as well.

Since Python is going to be used in machine learning in many cases, resources like NumPy and matplotlib are going to be used in many cases in order to help out with some of the modelings that we need to do with machine learning and to ensure that we are able to work with these technologies either.

The idea that we are going to get with this one is that the programmer is able to access these libraries in order to handle some of the key tasks that are inside of the bigger environment that we have with Python. It is then able to go through and integrate the results with all of the other elements and features of the program for machine learning, a neural network, and some of the other more advanced options that we would like to use.

You will also find that some of the utility that we are able to see with this library, as well as with the NumPy library is going to be centered around numbers. The utility of Matplotlib is going to be specifically done with visual plotting tools. So, in a sense, these resources are going t be more analytical rather than generative. However, all of the infrastructures that we are able to see with this library is going to allow for the programs of machine learning, when we use them in the proper manner, are able to give us the right results for human handlers as well.

With some of this information in mind, we need to look a bit more about the Matplotlib library in more detail. To start with, this is going to be part of the package from Python in order to help with 2D graphics. Learning how to work with this kind of library in an efficient manner is going to be so important when you would like to handle some of the visuals and more that you want to do in a data science project.

What is Matplotlib?

This is going to be one of the best plotting libraries that you are able to use in Python, especially when you would like to handle things like 2D graphics. It can be used with a lot of other different places, like on the web application servers, Python shell, Python script, and some of the other toolkits out there that are graphical user interfaces.

There are going to be a number of toolkits that are available that will help to extend out some of the functionality that we are going to see with matplotlib and will ensure that we are able to do some more with this program in no time at all. Some of these are going to include us going through a separate download, and then others are going to be found with the source code of this library but will have to depend on a few other aspects that are not found in Python or in this library. Some of the different extensions that we are able to focus on and can really work with when it is time to extend out what matplotlib is able to do will include:

1. Basemap: This is going to be a map plotting toolkit that can be helpful if this is what you would like to work with inside of your project. It is a good option to use if you would like to work with political boundaries, coastlines, and even some map projections overall.

2. Natgrid: This is going to be an interface that goes to the natgrid library. This is best when we want to handle something like the irregular gridding of the spaced data that we have.

3. Mplot3d: This is going to be helpful when you would like to extend out the 2D functions of matplotlib into something that is more 3D in nature instead.

4. Excel tools; This library is going to provide us with some of the utilities that we need in order to exchange data with Microsoft Excel if we need it.
5. Cartopy: This is going to be one of the mapping libraries that we are able to work with that are going to help us with some of the definitions of map projections and some of the arbitrary point, line, polygon, and image transformation capabilities to name a few of the features that we are able to rely on.

There are a lot of the different options that we are able to work with along the way in order to handle some of the features of this library as well. it is good for handling most of the features that we would like to see, and most of the graphs that are going to be important when it comes to this kind of data science. For example, you may find that this library is going to work well when we want to handle things like pie charts, line graphs, histograms, bar graphs, area plots, scatter plots, and more.

If you need to create your own chart or graph to go through some of the data that you are handling during this time, then working with the Matplotlib library is going to be one of the best options. It does lack some of the 3D features that you may need, so this is something to consider based on your data.   But for some of the basic parts that you would like to add into the mix, and for most of the visuals that you would like to focus on, you will find that the Matplotlib library is going to be able to handle it in no time.

Chapter 9: A Look at Data Mining

While we are here, we need to take some time to look at another process that is going to be so important to some of the work that we are trying to do with data science and more. You will find that there are so many different parts that come with this process, and data mining is going to be able to help us get it all done in no time at all. That is why we are going to spend some time exploring this wonderful topic of data mining in more depth, to help us really see what we are able to do with it and to help us make some important decisions as well.

To start with, we need to take a look at what data mining is all about. Data mining, to keep things simple, is going to be the process that is used by companies and other organizations in order to turn some of the raw data into information that is more useful. By using a variety of tools and software, including some of the data science and machine learning that we have already explored, we are able to look for patterns in some of the large batches of data that we have. And this is going to really help a business out.

For example, when the business is able to work with data mining, and they can find some of the important patterns that are found in the large batches of data, businesses are able to learn more about their customers, allowing them to develop some better marketing strategies, increase sales, and even cut down on some of the costs. But for all of this to work, we have to work with the idea of computer processing, warehousing, and even collecting the right data as we go along as well.

A Look at How Data Mining Works

The first thing that we need to take a look at is how data mining works. We will find that the processes of data mining are going to be what we can use in order to build up the models of machine learning that help power applications. This can include some of the website recommendation programs that we see on a regular basis and some of the technology that is found behind the major search engines that we use.

Data mining as a whole is going to involve the process of exploring and analyzing some big blocks of information with the goal of gleaning some meaningful patterns and trends along the way. It can then be used in many different ways, depending on what the company is hoping to do with it. For example, some of the ways that the information from data mining is being used today is to help them figure out the sentiment of their own customers, email filtering, fraud detection, credit risk management, and event marketing.

This process is going to have a few different steps, but the process is meant to break it down a bit so that we can understand what is going on and how we are able to use this for some of our own needs. For example, there are five main steps that we are able to focus on in order to get the data mining process to work and to ensure that we are going to understand what is going on the whole time.

The first step in the data mining process is where companies are going to collect data and can then load it up into their own data warehouses to use later. Then the company will be able to store and manage the data, which means that they will hold is somewhere safe, which is often done in the cloud. Management teams, IT professionals, and business analysts are going to be able to access the data in a variety of manners in order to figure out the best way to organize all of this.

And then we get to the final step where the application software is going to sort the data based on the results from the users. Then the end-user is able to present the data in a manner that is easy to share, which can include something like the graph or tables that we talked about before. In fact, much of this process is going to mirror what we are able to see when we talk about data science in general.

Handling Data Warehousing and the Mining Software We Need

Most of the data-mining programs that we are going to work with are responsible for analyzing the patterns and the relationships that are found in data based on what the user is requesting in the first place. For example, a company may choose to use this kind of software to help them create some new classes of information.

A good way to look at this is if a restaurant would like to work with data mining in order to help them figure out when they should use their specials. It would have to look at a ton of information to figure out what is selling well, what times are best, and more. For example, this restaurant is most likely going to look at the information that it has been able to collect and then will create some new classes based on when they see their customers visit, and what these customers order in the process.

In some other situations, these data miners are going to find some clusters of information that is based on logical relationships, or they will look at some of the sequential patterns and associations so that they are able to draw some conclusions about trends that are showing up in the behavior of the consumer.

While we are on the topic, we need to be able to take a look at the process of warehousing because it is an important part that comes with data mining. Warehousing, to keep it simple, is going to be when a company is able to centralize their data onto one database or one program. When we have our own data warehouse, we are able to spin off some segments of the data to specific users so that this can be analyzed and changed and used in any manner that is appropriate at the time.

This is not always going to be the case, though. We may find that in some situations, the analyst is going to start out with the data that they want, maybe they already went through and did the research to get things started.

But now they want to take that data and create a data warehouse based on that information. No matter how the entity, or the business, spend time organizing the data, they are going to use it in a manner to support the decision making process for management and others who are in charge.

An Example of Data Mining

The final thing that we are going to take some time to look at in this part of the guidebook is an example of how this data mining process is going to work for us. Keep in mind that there are a lot of these that we are able to work with, and it often depends on what the customer wants, and how they would like to work with some of the data that they have.

For our example, we are going to take a look at some of the grocery stores in our area. How many times have you gone into one and seen that they offer loyalty cards to customers who would like to use them? You may even have some of your own as well, depending on the incentives that are given and what stores you like to visit. These loyalty cards are going to give you some access to a lot of benefits, and they are a really well-known option of data mining when we look at the techniques.

These are interesting because they are going to provide some benefits to both of the parties involved. The company is going to be able to gather up the information that they want on their customers, or at least the customers who have these cards and use them, and the customers will usually get points, special deals, or something else when they choose to use the loyalty cards. This is a great way for the company to really get more data in no time.

These loyalty cards are great for the customer in many manners. For example, it is going to provide them with some benefits in order to keep them coming back. Often it is going to include something like prices that are reduced and that other non-members are not able to gain access to. The type of incentive is going to change based on what we see that the company would like to work with.

But the company is going to benefit from these as well. for example, they are a great way for the store to keep track of who is buying what, when they are buying it, and at what price they are more likely to make that purchase as well. That is a ton of data at the fingertips of those who are doing this kind of thing and can be valuable to any business. In fact, there are a lot of businesses that are not in retail or in the food industry who would like to be able to work with something like this in order to reach their customers, keep the customers coming back, and have all of the data that they need to complete the data science project that they would like all rolled up into one as well.

After the company has had some time to gather up all of the data, they are able to move on to the process of analyzing the data. Once the analysis is done, they are able to then use the data to make sure that they are serving the customers even more and still increasing their profits. For example, this data could help the stores to offer coupons to their customers that are more targeted to the buying habits of that customer, and it can even help the store to decide what items they are going to list for sale at different times of the year, and which ones they are going to set at full price.

All of this is going to be done in order to help the company to get some of the results that they would like out of this process. They can gather up that data and learn as much about the customers as possible, while still providing a good incentive to the customers to come back and use the cards again. This is the perfect way for the company to gather the information that they need for a good data analysis and will ensure that both parties are going to win in the long run.

Data mining can cause some concerns in some situations. This is going to cause some concerns when the company chooses to only work with the selected information that they want and not the kind that is going to be representative of the overall sample group. This is often going to be done in order to prove the hypothesis or the ideas that the person had when they got started, and it is going to hurt the end result that you are able to get overall.

If you really want to learn about your customers and what they are able to provide to you in terms of valuable information so that you can serve them better, you need to leave some of the preconceived notions and biases at the door. If you are only using a small sample size of what is there, and not really focusing on what is important in the data that you work with, then you are not going to serve yourself or your customers all that well.

We have spent some time taking a look at some of the things that you are able to do when it is time to work with data analysis and complete your data science project. It is going to be so important to follow data mining in the right manner because it is going to lead you to some of the success that you would like to do in this process.

Keep in mind a few key points before you move on and work with some of the other topics that we have in this guidebook. These will include:

1. Data mining as a whole, and as a process, is going to be where we take the necessary steps in order to process and analyze a large amount of information. All o this data is going to be used to help us discern some of the patterns and trends that we need to make smart decisions about our data.

2. Data mining can be used by companies for everything from learning about what the customers are the most interested in, or what

these customers are the most likely to buy from your company or any other company out there so that you can tailor the experience, and the products that you release, to some of these wants and needs as well.

3. And the data mining programs that you are going to use are useful because they are able to break down some of the connections and the patterns that are found in the data. And this is based on what information your users or customers are providing or requesting at the time.

As we can see here, there are a lot of benefits that are going to come from using data mining as an important part of the whole data science process. When we are able to put all of these parts together and use them in the proper manner as well, we will be able to make sure that we find the right data, put it in the right warehouse for everyone to use, and so much more. Following the steps in this guidebook will ensure that you are able to get it all done in no time.

Chapter 10: The Seaborn Library

Another library that we need to take a look at here is going to be the Seaborn library. This is another library that is great to use when it is time to do some data visualization in Python. This library is going to be built on top of the Matplotlib library that we talked about before, so we need to make sure that we have a good understanding of both of these to get them to work. And Seaborn is going to offer a lot of the advanced capabilities that we need with data visualizations in order to help us get the work done.

Though this library is able to help us draw up a lot of the charts that we need, including regression plots, grid plots, and matrix plots, we are also going to spend some time looking at more of the things that you are able to do with this library such as drawing categorical and distributional plots. With this in mind, let's take a look at some of the different parts that we would like to handle when it comes time to work on the Seaborn Library.

How to Download the Seaborn Library

The first thing that we need to take some time to look at in this chapter is the process that we need to use in order to download this library. There are going to be a few methods that we are able to use in order to get this done. First, if you would like to work with the pip installer that comes with Python, then you would just need to work with the command below to get this library downloaded and ready to go:

pip install seaborn

in addition, if you are choosing to download things with the help of the Anaconda distribution that comes with Python, you would need to work with the coding below in order to help you get this Seaborn library downloaded and ready to go for our needs:

conda install seaborn

The Dataset

Now that we have the library downloaded and ready to go (and wasting that really easy to work with?), it is time to handle some of the data sets that we are able to work with. The dataset that we are going to spend some of our time working on in this part is to draw our plots with the Titanic dataset. This is going to be a dataset that is automatically downloaded along with the Seaborn library when we do some of the steps that were above. All that you need to do to make this happen is to work with the function of load_dataset and then pass it the name of the dataset as well.

To start with this part, we need to take a look at what the data set Titanic is going to look like overall. We are able to use the coding below to help us work with this one

```
import pandas as pd
import numpy as np

import matplotlib.pyplot as plt
import seaborn as sns

dataset = sns.load_dataset('titanic')

dataset.head()
```

In this coding, we are going to be able to work with some of the different libraries that we need, and not just the seaborn library. This one is going to be built upon some of the other libraries that are important with Python and data science. In particular, we are going to take a look at how we need to import Pandas, NumPy, and Seaborn as well.

When we execute the script above, we are going to load up the dataset Titanic, and it is going to display for us the first five rows of the set using the head function. You can execute this and see what the first five rows of it are going to look like. The set of data is going to contain 891 rows and 15 columns and will have a lot of o information about the passengers who boarded the Titanic ship.

The original task that we are going to work with here is to go through and predict whether or not the passenger was able to survive the shipwreck based on a lot of different features. We are able to look at things like the ticket, the class of ticket, the ag of the passenger, the gender, the cabin they were in and more. This will all help to tell us whether someone was likely to have survived the Titanic or not. We will find that the Seaborn library is going to be a good one to use because it will help us to find some of the patterns that we need in all of that data, as well.

The Distributional Plots

The next thing on the list that we need to focus on is the distributional plots. As we can guess with the name, these are going to be types of plots that are there to show us the statistical distribution of the data. That is why we are going to spend some time in this section looking at some of the most common out of these distribution plots that we are able to handle in Seaborn.

First on the list is going to be the Dist Plot. This is going to be written out as a distplot() and is going to show the histogram distribution of data for a single column. The column name, when we get to this point, is going to be passed as the parameter to the function of distplot(). So, we are going to use this in order to see how the price of a ticket for each passenger is going to be distributed. We are able to use the following script to check out what this distribution was.

sns.distplot(dataset['fare'])

Take a bit of time and look at executing this code in your compiler. You should see that most of the tickets for this ride were somewhere between 0 and 50 dollars each. The line that you will see show up is going to represent the kernel density estimation. You can decide to take this line out bypassing the false as the parameters for the kde distribution, and using the code below:

Sns.distplot(dataset['fare'] kde=False)

When you do this, you will be able to notice that there is no longer a line for the kernel density estimation on that plot. Another thing that we can spend some time on with this library is the bins parameter. This one is going to be good because it allows us to choose which details we would like to have shown up in the graph, and we can even choose whether we would like to see more or fewer details in our graph. A good code to use for this one includes the following:

Sns.distplot(dataset['fare'] kde=False, bins=10)

Here we are going to be able to set the number of bins that we are working with to ten, but you can definitely go through and pick out another set of bins that works the best for your needs as well. When we do this and execute, we will find that for more than 700 of the passengers on the Titanic, their ticket price fell between 0 and 50.

Then we are able to move on to what is known as the joint plot. We are going to write out this function as jointplot(), and it is used in order to display some of the mutual distribution that comes with each column. You will have to make sure that there are three main parameters that are going to show up in order to pass with this one.

The first parameter that we are going to notice is the column name. This can be anything you would like, but remember that it is going to display more about the distribution of data on the x-axis. The second parameter is going to be the column name that you would like to use, which is going to display the distribution of data on our y-axis. And the third important parameter is going to be the name that is on the data frame for itself.

With some of this in mind, we are going to spend some time doing a joint plot. Our goal is to do one of the age and the fare columns to help us figure out whether there are some relationships present between both of these.

The code that we are able to use to get this one to work will include:

```
sns.jointplot(x = 'age', y = 'fare', data=datasect)
```

Take a moment to type this into your compiler and see what is going to come out. From this output, you are able to see the three parts that show up in the joint plot that we are working with. These three parts are going to include the distribution plot that is needed at the top for the column we are working with on the x-axis, the distribution plot that will fall over to the right for the column that is on the y-axis, and then there is going to be a scatter plot that shows up in between both of these as well. This scatter plot is important because it helps us to see the mutual distribution of the data for both of the other two columns that we are talking about. You can see with this one that there really isn't a correlation present between the fares that the passengers spent and their ages.

Now, this is not the only thing that we are able to do here to get some good results. We are able to also change up the joint plot type by passing a value for the kind parameter if we would lie. For example, if you would like to work with something other than a scatter plot, and you would like to make sure that you are able to display the distribution of data in the form of a plot that is hexagonal, then you would have to pass on the hex instead of the kind parameter. The script that is going to help us to get this done is the following:

sns.jointplot(x = 'age', y = 'fare', data = dataset, kind = 'hex')

When we are working with this hexagonal plot, the hexagon with the most points will get the color that is darker. So, if you execute the code that is above, and you look at the graph, then you are going to see that most of the passengers that we are dealing with on the Titanic were somewhere between the ages of 20 and 30, and most of these individuals paid somewhere between 10 and 50 dollars to get on the boat.

The next thing that we want to take a look at is the pair plot and how this one is going to work for our needs. This one is going to be written out as pairplot(). This one is going to be the plot that will help us to plot out a joint plot for all of the potential combinations of Boolean and numeric columns that are found in the set of data. You will only need to pass the name of the set of data as the parameter over to the function and to do that; we are going to work with the coding below:

sns.pairplot(dataset)

Note with this one that before you spend some time executing that script, you need to make sure that all of the values that are considered null are taken out of the set of data. The best way to help us get all of this done and to ensure that the work is going to look the way that we want is to work with the following code

dataset = dataset.dropna().

Then we will see from the output of the pair plot that there will be a list, and lots of diagrams, about all of the joint plots for the Boolean and the numeric columns that are in the set of data for Titanic right now. It is also possible for us to go through and add in some of the information that we need from the categorical column over to the pair plot. To make sure that this is happening, you are able to pass the name of the categorical column over to the hue parameter. For example, if you would like to plot some of the information about the gender of those on board over to the pair plot, then we would need to work with the script below to get this done:

Sns.pairplot(dataset, hue = 'sex')

When we do the output, you are going to be able to see some of the information about the males, and this is going to show up in arranging in the data we are using, and the females and their information is going to show up in blue. This is going to be something that you and others who work with this kind of coding will be able to see from the legend that shows up as well. from the joint plot on the top left, you will be able to see that out of the passengers who survived, the majority of them are female, which is what we would expect out of this in the first place.

Then we are able to move on to what is known as the rug plot. We are able to work with this function, and it looks like rugplot(). This one is a good option to use when it is time to draw up some of the small bars along the x-axis for each point that shows up in the set of data. To help us plot this rug plot, we have to make sure that we are passing over the name of the column. In the code below, we are going to plot the rug plot for the fare of those who got on the Titanic:

```
sns.rugplot(dataset['fare])
```

From this output, we are going to see something that is similar to what we saw with the distplot() that we talked about earlier. This code is going to show us that most of the instances of the fare are going to end up with values that are between 0 and 100.

And there we have it for some of the most commonly used distribution plots that are found in this Seaborn Library from Python. S we can see already, there are a lot of times when we are able to use these to help us get better results and really see what some of the information is telling us. And with that in mind, we need to take a look at a few of the categorical plots that this Seaborn library is able to bring to us as well.

The Categorical Plots

The next type of plot that we need to explore when it comes to working with the Seaborn library is the categorical plots. These are going to be the kind that we are able to use when it is time to plot data that is categorical in nature. In these kinds of plots, the values in the categorical columns are going to be plotted against another categorical or numeric column. There are a number of options that fit into this kind of thing, and we are going to take some time to look at them now.

The first option on our list is the bar plot, which we are able to write out as a barplot(). This one is going to be used in order to display for us the mean value for each of the values that show up in our categorical columns and will compare it against one of the numeric columns as well.

The first parameter that we are going to see here is known as the categorical column. Then we have the second parameter that is going to be the numeric column that we were talking about. And finally, the third parameter that we need to focus on is going to be the set of data. For example, if you would like to be able to know the mean value of the passengers, whether just the males, just the females, or some other combination, you would want to work with the bar plot. The best code to getting this taken care of will include:

```
sns.barplot(x = 'sex', y = 'age', data = dataset)
```

When we take a look at the output that comes with this one, you can see that the average age of the males who were on the ship is just a bit younger than 40. But the average age of the female passengers is going to end up being around 33 instead.

In addition to spending some time finding the average, the bar plot is also something that we are able to use to calculate some of the other aggregate values from each of the categories that are there. To make this happen, we also need to pass the aggregate function over to our estimator. For example, you are able to calculate the standard deviation for the age of each gender, and we are able to do this with the following code:

```
import numpy as np

import matplotlib.pyplot as plt
import seaborn as sns

sns.barplot(x = 'sex', y = 'age', data = dataset,
estimator.std)
```

Notice in the script that we worked with above that we spent some time working with the std aggregate function from the NumPy library in order to calculate the standard deviation for the ages of male and female passengers. Take a moment to look at the output that you are going to see with this one.

From there, we are able to work with the count plot. This is going to look very similar to what we were working with on the bar plot. But you will find that it is going to display the count of the categories in a specific column that we are working with. For example, if we would like to take some time to count the number of women and male passengers to see if there were more of either gender or not, then we would be able to do this with the count plot. The code that we are able to use in order to make this happen includes:

sns.countplot(x = 'sex', data=dataset)

Then we are able to work with the box plot. This is going to be used in order to display the distribution that we have of the categorical data in the form of quartiles that can make it easier to see some of the information that we need. The center of the box is going to show us the median value that we need. The value that is then going to show up in the lower whisker all the way to the bottom of our box is going to become our first quartile.

And then we are able to go to the bottom of the box up to about the halfway point, and this is going to be known as the second quartile that we have. From the middle of the box to the top of the box is going to be the third quartile. And then the top of our box all the way to the top whisker that we have is going to be the last quartile that we can work with.

With this one in mind, we are able to go through and plot out the box plot that will display the distribution for the age, and this will be done with respect to each gender. You will need to first pass the categorical column as the first parameter, which is sex in this case, and then the numeric column, which is going to be the age, as our second parameter. And then, we are able to pass over the set of data that we have as the third parameter. To make all of this happen, we need to take a look at the script that is below:

```
sns.boxplot( x = 'sex', y = 'age', data = dataset)
```

Execute this one, and then we are able to take a look at what some of these means, and how we are able to use this for some of our needs as well. We are going to take a look at just the females to start. The first quartile is going to start around 5 here and will end at 22. This means that about 25 percent of our passengers are going to be somewhere between the age of 5 and 25 at the time of sailing. Then we will see that the second quartile is going to start around the age of 23, and will end around the age of 32. This means that another 25 percent of the passengers fell between these two ages.

Then we are able to look at the third quartile and find that it starts and ends between 34 and 42, which means that another 25 percent of the passengers are going to fit into this age range. And the final and last quartile, the fourth one, is going to start around the age of 43 and ends around the age of 65.

If you find that there are any outliers or groups of passengers that are not going to fit into these quartiles all that well, they are going to be known as outliers, and they will be represented with a dot on the box plot that you are going to be working with here.

You are able to add and take away anything that you would like to make these box plots more functional for some of the work that you are trying to do. Often, one of the ways that you are able to make these fancier, for example, is by adding in another layer of distribution for it. For example, if you would like to see whether the box plots of the age of passengers for both of the genders, and you would also like to have some information about whether these people survived or not, you are able to pass on survived as the value to our hue parameter as we will show in the code we are working with below:

```
sns.boxplot( x = 'sex', y = 'age', data = dataset, hut = "survived")
```

Now, in addition to the information about how old all of the genders are, you can also see a good idea of the distribution of those passengers who ended up surviving. For instance, we are able to see that among the male passengers, on average more of those who were younger survived compared to those who were older. In addition, we are able to get a look at the variation among the age of the female passengers who did not survive is much greater than the age of the surviving females.

Another option to take a look at is known as the violin plot. This one is going to be similar to what we see with the box plot, but it is going to allow us to display all of the components that actually correspond to the data point. This function, written out as violinplot(), will be used to plot this as well. Similar to what we see with the box plot, the first parameter is going to be the categorical column, the second parameter is the numeric column, and then the third parameter is going to be the set of data that we are able to work with here.

With this in mind, we are going to take a moment to look at an example of the code that you can write for the violin plot. We are going to plot one of these that is able to display the distribution of age in respect to each of the genders that we have:

sns.violinplot(x = 'sex', y = 'age', data = dataset)

You are able to also see from the figure above that this kind of plot is going to provide us with a lot more information about the data compared to what we see with the box plot. Instead of plotting out the quartiles, the violin plot is going to allow us to see all of the components that are actually going to correspond to the data. The area where this plot is thicker on the graph is going to show us the higher number of instances for that age. In this one, in the plot for males, it is going to be really evident that the number of passengers between the ages of 20 and 40 is much higher than what we see with the rest of the ages that we can use.

Similar to the box plots that we are able to work with, it is possible to go through and add in some other categorical variables to this plat. We are able to make it happen using the hue parameter that we had before. The code that we would need to use to make this one work includes:

sns.violinplot(x = 'sex', y = 'age', data = dataset, hue = 'survived')

This part is going to tell us a lot of information on the violin plot. For example, we are able to take a look at the bottom of the violin plot for those males who were able to survive, which is on the left in orange. You will find that it is a bit thicker than the bottom of the violin plot for the males who didn't survive, which is the left in blue. This means that the number of younger male passengers who survived is greater than the number of young male passengers who did not survive. This kind of plot is going to be able to show us a lot of information on the downside as well, and it is going to take a bit of time and some effort in order to look through these and really see what is being done.

Instead of taking time to plot two different graphs for the passengers who survived and those who were not able to survive, you can have one of these violin plots get divided into two halves. One half is going to represent surviving, and then the other is going to represent the passengers who are not going to survive. To do this, you need to be able to pass the True as a value for the split parameter of the function of the violin plot(). The code that we are able to use in order to make this work for our needs will be below:

sns.violinplot(x = 'sex', y = 'age', data = dataset, hue = 'survived', split=True)

When we do this one, we are able to clearly see the comparison between the age of the passengers who survived and who did not when we work with both the males and females. Both the box plots and the violin plot are going to be useful. But with a rule of thumb here is that if you would like to be able to present your data to an audience that is not technical in nature, then the box plot is the one that you should work with because they are easier to comprehend overall.

But, on the other hand, if you are trying to do something a little bit differently, and you would like to present some of the results that you have to a research community, it is going to be more convenient to work with the violin plot. The reason for this is that it is going to help save us some space and will make it so that we are able to convey more of the information that we want in less time overall.

We took some time to look at a lot of the different things that we are able to do when it is time to handle Python and the Seaborn library for our needs. These are all going to be important parts of the process to work with because they allow us the option to really do some of the work that we need, and really learn how we can understand some of the plots and the points that we are working with as well.

There are a lot of other things that we are able to do when it is time to handle the visuals of this process and more, and that is why we took some time to look more at the Seaborn library overall. When you need to get a better look at some of the information that is out there about your dataset, and you want to be able to fully understand what is going on with it, make sure to check out this guidebook to help you get started right away!

Chapter 11: The Real-Life Applications of Data Science

Now that we have had some time to take a look at how data science is going to work, it is time for us to go through and look at a different angle when it comes to this data science. We have the basics and the steps ready to go, but it is time to learn how this kind of method and the process of data science can be used in the real world.

There are already a lot of businesses out there who are working with data science and enjoying the benefits that come with this one overall. And your business is able to do this as well. it just takes a bit of time and dedication in order to figure out the method that you would like to use for your own needs. Some of the real-life applications that we are going to see when we are ready to take the knowledge that we have learned about data science in this guidebook and put it to good use will include:

Helps Us to Understand Our Customers

One of the best reasons to work with data science at all, and to go through some of the steps that we talked about in this guidebook, is to use it to help us understand our customers a little bit better. For most companies, the more that they are able to understand their customers and make sure that they are going to like your products will be the key that we need to have in order to do really well with some of the marketing that we choose to focus on.

There are a lot of diverse people who are a part of your customer base, and you have to make sure that you are providing information and advertisements that are going to fit in well with what speaks to them, and will bring them into your store. And working with data science is going to be the best way to group your customers into their own clusters to know who to market to, what they will respond to, and even if there are some new niches out there that you are able to market to as well.

We have to spend our time marketing to different groups of people based on how they will react to our message, and how much we think they are going to be in our target group. You would advertise and market to people in their 40s in a different manner than you would to those who are in their 20s, so knowing your customers can help you make sure that you are reaching the target market in the right manner.

Through some of the techniques of machine learning and more, especially with clustering, we are able to see where the majority of our customers will lie, which is going to help us when it is time to make a new campaign. You may find that the information validates some of the beliefs that you already had along the way, and sometimes the ideas are going to be brand-new. Either way, this is going to be a great way for you to ensure that you are on the right track when you begin.

Another interesting thing that comes up with this one is that we can use this to help us look at some of the outliers. In many cases, these outliers are not going to be all that important. They will just be some extra cases that we will cut out to help keep the algorithm working well. But in other situations, if there are a substantial number of them, and they tend to cluster around the same mid-point, then this could tell you some good information. It could tell us some more about a new niche of customers that we are able to work with, which can open up a lot of possibilities as well.

Can Give Us a Leg Up On the Competition

Many companies are going to work with the idea of data science in order to help them gain a leg up on the competition overall. This allows them a chance to go through and really make sure that they are able to beat out the competition, and that they will be able to think of new and innovative ways to reach the customer.

When you are in a market where there is a lot of competition, and there isn't a lot of room for error or reaching out of the niche, you need to make sure that you are providing the customers with a good reason to pick you rather than someone else. And the more competition that we gain in this modern world, the harder it is to really see some of the results that we need as a result as well. The more that we are able to differentiate ourselves from the competition, the better our sales will be.

There are a lot of different methods that we are able to use in order to make sure that our business is able to beat out the competition. We can find new methods to use to make our products that reduce the costs. We can find new products that are going to work well on the market and will provide us with some of the best sales. We can learn more about our customers and where to find them so that our marketing efforts are a little bit better. And we can even use it to find some new niche to reach, one that maybe the competition has not learned about yet, and that can help us as well.

The point here is that data science is able to help us with all of this. It can show us how to beat out the competition in general, or it can help us if we are looking at one of the parts above in particular. If you collect the right data and go through the different steps that are listed with this one already, you will find that it is easy to find the exact way that you can beat out the competition and see some of the results that you would like.

A Great Way to Cut Down on Waste

Every business, no matter what industry they are in or what they sell and produce, will end up with some waste that they need to work with. This waste is going to cost the business a lot of money and will cut into their bottom line. There is only so much that they are able to charge for the item, so if there is a lot of unnecessary waste, that means that it is going to cut into the profits that we are able to make.

Data science is able to help us out with this problem a bit. We will be able to go through and work on cutting down on some of the waste that we are working with in order to see some of the results that we would like too. And data science, when it is fed the right information, is going to be able to really look at some of the information, and tell us exactly where the waste is.

When this process is used in the right manner, we will be able to find some of the best ways to cut down on some of the waste that we are dealing with. This is going to make life a little bit easier when it is time to keep the waste down to a minimum, increases profits, and could end up helping us provide a higher quality product to our customers.

You may even be surprised about some of the types of waste that you are able to find in your own business. You may not realize that there is a faster method of getting the work done. Or maybe you can learn the best times to fix your machines, and make predictions on when a part is going to fail, rather than just having that machine break down in production and cost you time and money You could use it in order to cut down on how long a process takes, how many steps that are done in the process, and more.

The trick here is to make sure that you are cutting down on the waste in a manner that is going to improve the product or at least maintain the quality that is already on the product. If you find a way that could reduce the amount of time and money that it takes to make the product, but it results in a lower quality product, then this is not a method that you should use.

Makes It Easier to Figure Out What Products to Release

In the past, working with your products and knowing which ones you should release, and which ones would fail when it was time to do a release, was hard. You could do a little bit of market research, but often this was going to be behind the curve. You are able to figure out the products that the customers are already using or what they may like now. But figuring out what trends are happening in the future, and where we are able to meet the customer in the future is going to be a bit of a challenge.

This was something that a lot of businesses had to face in the past. They may make guesses about the best products to release, and sometimes they were right, though it was a big risk, and they were often wrong. But with the help of data science, we are able to cut out some of the risks, and we can better ensure that we are picking out the best products to work with, the ones that are going to help us to see some good results, ones that are likely to be successful in no time at all.

When we use data science, we are able to learn more about our customers and what they are looking for overall. We are able to learn about what products are out there, what trends are going to show up in the future, and ore. Then when we complete the process, all the way from gathering the data through to when we read and understand the data at the end, we will know with certainty which products are going to be a hit and which ones won't.

There are a lot of companies who have been able to work with this option and figure out what they should release next. This helps them to cut down some of the risks that are out there and will ensure that we are actually releasing some of the products that our customers want and will actually purchase as well.

Best Way to Make Decisions for Your Business

Making decisions for any business is going to be quite tough. There are so many variables that are going to come into play, and it is not always going to work out the way that you would like. There is also a good deal of risk that is going to show up when it is time to handle these decisions, and the fear of losing a lot of money or making a big mistake is enough to make anyone a bit worried and frazzled, especially if they do not have a lot of experience to start with.

When we work with data science, the process of making decisions is going to be so much easier. We are able to take a look at the problem from a lot of different angles. And we have the option of using a lot of data, some good algorithms, and a few other steps, in order to point us in the right direction. For example, when we take some time to add the data science that we are talking about with some predictive analysis, it is much easier to figure out what is the most likely outcome based on the data we have, and the course of action that we are trying to follow.

Think about how nice it would be in order to make a decision and know that it is not going to be the wrong one. Think about how you would feel if you were able to make decisions that were based on data, without having to guess and hope that the decisions that you make were the right ones. The idea of using data science in order to make some of the big decisions in your business is a great way to get some of the data in there, and that ensures that all of the decisions that you make are secure and safe.

Even for people who have been in their industries for a longer period of time, and who have some experience with the process as well, making decisions is going to be a challenge in some cases. But with the help of data science, the right data, and some strong algorithms to help get it all done, you will be able to get things to work out in the manner that will help guarantee the success that you would like.

As we can see, there are a lot of ways that we are able to use data science on a regular basis. Being able to learn how to work with this and getting it to work for some of your needs is important. Luckily, there is a ton of data out there that we are able to work with, which is going to make things so much easier for us to handle. And when we are able to put all of these things together, and we learn more about the steps of data science, we are going to be able to see all of the great results overall.

Conclusion

Thank you for making it through to the end of *Python for Data Science*, let's hope it was informative and able to provide you with all of the tools you need to achieve your goals whatever they may be.

The next step is to start learning how to work with the process of data science for some of your own needs as well. There are already a lot of companies out there who work in a wide variety of fields and industries along the way, who are working with data science. They have already found that there are a ton of benefits that come with using this kind of process, and your company will be able to learn how to work with this as well. That is why this guidebook spent some time talking more about data science and all of the great parts that are going to come with it along the way, as well.

The beginning of this guidebook spent some time looking at all of the great parts that come with data science. We are not able to work with the process of data science if we don't understand how it works in the first place. We spent some time exploring what data science is all about, who can use data science, the benefits of data science, and even some of the parts of the data science lifecycle. This helps us to see just how involved this process is, and why we need to work not just with the analysis, but also with the proper gathering, organization, cleaning, and more of the data that we have.

After this part, we are going to take some time to look at some of the other features and ore that we are able to use along the way with this data science project. We are going to explore a bit about how the Python language fits into this mix, the importance of machine learning and how it can help us to set ourselves up to be successful with writing out our own models and algorithms to handle the data, and a bit more about a predictive analysis and how this can be combined in to help us make some good predictions about the data that we are working with.

And finally, we will spend some of our time looking at the different libraries that we are able to use to make this process a little bit better. We will find that there are a ton of libraries that we are able to add to Python to ensure that we are going to get the best results. There are a ton of options that we are able to work with when it is time to handle some of our data science projects and will ensure that we are able to learn more about our customers and our market in order to get the most success.

Many companies are going to use the ideas of data science in order to get as many benefits as possible. Each company will be able to use this in a different manner and will find that it can help them add to their bottom line, increase profits, and really reach their customers in new and innovative manners. When you re ready to learn more about how data science works, and all of the different parts that come with it, make sure to check out this guidebook to get started.

Finally, if you found this book useful in any way, a review on Amazon is always appreciated!